Soon To Be Mr. & Mrs.

VERLING

Wedding Date:

Wedding Planner

WEDDING DATE & TIME:

VENUE ADDRESS:

BUDGET:

OFFICIANT:

WEDDING PARTY:

NOTES & REMINDERS:

TO DO LIST:

Wedding Budget Planner

	TOTAL COST:	DEPOSIT:	REMAINDER:
WEDDING VENUE			
RECEPTION VENUE			
FLORIST			
OFFICIANT			
CATERER			
WEDDING CAKE			
BRIDAL ATTIRE			
GROOM ATTIRE			
BRIDAL JEWELRY			
BRIDESMAID ATTIRE			
GROOMSMEN ATTIRE			
HAIR & MAKE UP			
PHOTOGRAPHER			
VIDEOGRAPHER			
DJ SERVICE/ENTERTAINMENT			
INVITATIONS			
TRANSPORTATION			
WEDDING PARTY GIFTS			
RENTALS			
HONEYMOON			

12 Months Before

- SET THE DATE
- SET YOUR BUDGET
- CHOOSE YOUR THEME
- ORGANIZE ENGAGEMENT PARTY
- RESEARCH VENUES
- BOOK A WEDDING PLANNER
- RESEARCH PHOTOGRAPHERS
- RESEARCH ~~VIDEOGRAPHERS~~
- RESEARCH DJ'S/ENTERTAINMENT

- CONSIDER FLORISTS
- RESEARCH CATERERS
- DECIDE ON OFFICIANT JR?.
- CREATE INITIAL GUEST LIST
- CHOOSE WEDDING PARTY
- SHOP FOR WEDDING DRESS
- REGISTER WITH GIFT REGISTRY
- DISCUSS HONEYMOON IDEAS
- RESEARCH WEDDING RINGS

THINGS TO REMEMBER:

9 Months Before

FINALIZE GUEST LIST

ORDER INVITATIONS

PLAN YOUR RECEPTION

BOOK PHOTOGRAPHER

BOOK VIDEOGRAPHER

BOOK FLORIST

BOOK DJ/ENTERTAINMENT

BOOK CATERER

CHOOSE WEDDING CAKE
Cindy (Oakes) Jamie's Mom

CHOOSE WEDDING GOWN

ORDER BRIDESMAIDS DRESSES

RESERVE TUXEDOS

ARRANGE TRANSPORTATION

BOOK WEDDING VENUE

BOOK RECEPTION VENUE

PLAN HONEYMOON

BOOK OFFICIANT

BOOK ROOMS FOR GUESTS

THINGS TO REMEMBER:

6 Months Before

- ORDER THANK YOU NOTES
- REVIEW RECEPTION DETAILS
- MAKE APPT FOR DRESS FITTING
- CONFIRM BRIDEMAIDS DRESSES
- GET MARRIAGE LICENSE

- BOOK HAIR/MAKE UP STYLIST
- CONFIRM MUSIC SELECTIONS
- PLAN BRIDAL SHOWER *Maid of Honor*
- PLAN REHEARSAL
- SHOP FOR WEDDING RINGS

THINGS TO REMEMBER:

3 Months Before

MAIL OUT INVITATIONS

MEET WITH OFFICIANT

BUY GIFTS FOR WEDDING PARTY

BOOK FINAL GOWN FITTING

BUY WEDDING BANDS

PLAN YOUR HAIR STYLE

PURCHASE SHOES/HEELS

CONFIRM PASSPORTS ARE VALID

FINALIZE RECEPTION MENU

PLAN REHEARSAL DINNER

CONFIRM ALL BOOKINGS

APPLY FOR MARRIAGE LICENSE

CONFIRM MUSIC SELECTIONS

DRAFT WEDDING VOWS

CHOOSE YOUR MC

ARRANGE AIRPORT TRANSFER

THINGS TO REMEMBER:

1 Month Before

- [ ] CONFIRM FINAL GUEST COUNT
- [ ] CONFIRM RECEPTION DETAILS
- [ ] ATTEND FINAL GOWN FITTING
- [ ] CONFIRM PHOTOGRAPHER
- [ ] WRAP WEDDING PARTY GIFTS
- [ ] CREATE PHOTOGRAPHY SHOT LIST

- [ ] REHEARSE WEDDING VOWS
- [ ] BOOK MANI-PEDI
- [ ] CONFIRM WITH FLORIST
- [ ] CONFIRM VIDEOGRAPHER
- [ ] PICK UP BRIDEMAIDS DRESSES
- [ ] CREATE WEDDING SCHEDULE

THINGS TO REMEMBER:

1 Week Before

- FINALIZE SEATING PLANS
- MAKE PAYMENTS TO VENDORS
- PACK FOR HONEYMOON
- CONFIRM HOTEL RESERVATIONS
- GIVE SCHEDULE TO PARTY

- DELIVER LICENSE TO OFFICIANT
- CONFIRM WITH BAKERY
- PICK UP WEDDING DRESS
- PICK UP TUXEDOS
- GIVE MUSIC LIST TO DJ

THINGS TO REMEMBER:

1 Day Before

- [ ] GET MANICURE/PEDICURE
- [ ] ATTEND REHEARSAL DINNER
- [ ] GET A GOOD NIGHT'S SLEEP!
- [ ] GIVE GIFTS TO WEDDING PARTY
- [ ] FINALIZE PACKING

TO DO LIST:

The Big Day!

- GET HAIR & MAKE UP DONE
- HAVE A HEALTHY BREAKFAST
- ENJOY YOUR BIG DAY!

- MEET WITH BRIDESMAIDS
- GIVE RINGS TO BEST MAN

TO DO LIST:

Wedding Planner

ENGAGEMENT PARTY:

DATE: _____

LOCATION: _____

TIME: _____

NUMBER OF GUESTS: _____

NOTES:

BRIDAL SHOWER:

DATE: _____

LOCATION: _____

TIME: _____

NUMBER OF GUESTS: _____

NOTES:

STAG & DOE PARTY:

DATE: _____

LOCATION: _____

TIME: _____

NUMBER OF GUESTS: _____

NOTES:

Wedding Party

MAID/MATRON OF HONOR:

PHONE: _____ DRESS SIZE: _____ SHOE SIZE: _____

EMAIL: _____

BRIDESMAID:

PHONE: _____ DRESS SIZE: _____ SHOE SIZE: _____

EMAIL: _____

BRIDESMAID #2:

PHONE: _____ DRESS SIZE: _____ SHOE SIZE: _____

EMAIL: _____

BRIDESMAID #3:

PHONE: _____ DRESS SIZE: _____ SHOE SIZE: _____

EMAIL: _____

BRIDESMAID #4:

PHONE: _____ DRESS SIZE: _____ SHOE SIZE: _____

EMAIL: _____

NOTES:

Wedding Party

BEST MAN:

PHONE: _____ WAIST SIZE: _____ SHOE SIZE: _____

NECK SIZE: _____ SLEEVE SIZE: _____ JACKET SIZE: _____

EMAIL: _____

GROOMSMEN #1:

PHONE: _____ WAIST SIZE: _____ SHOE SIZE: _____

NECK SIZE: _____ SLEEVE SIZE: _____ JACKET SIZE: _____

EMAIL: _____

GROOMSMEN #2:

PHONE: _____ WAIST SIZE: _____ SHOE SIZE: _____

NECK SIZE: _____ SLEEVE SIZE: _____ JACKET SIZE: _____

EMAIL: _____

GROOMSMEN #3:

PHONE: _____ WAIST SIZE: _____ SHOE SIZE: _____

NECK SIZE: _____ SLEEVE SIZE: _____ JACKET SIZE: _____

EMAIL: _____

GROOMSMEN #4:

PHONE: _____ WAIST SIZE: _____ SHOE SIZE: _____

NECK SIZE: _____ SLEEVE SIZE: _____ JACKET SIZE: _____

EMAIL: _____

Photographer

PHOTOGRAPHER:

PHONE: .... COMPANY: ....

EMAIL: .... ADDRESS: ....

....

WEDDING PACKAGE OVERVIEW:

EST PRICE: ....

INCLUSIONS:	YES ✓	NO ✓	COST:
ENGAGEMENT SHOOT:			
PHOTO ALBUMS:			
FRAMES:			
PROOFS INCLUDED:			
NEGATIVES INCLUDED:			

TOTAL COST: ....

Videographer

VIDEOGRAPHER:

PHONE: _____   COMPANY: _____

EMAIL: _____   ADDRESS: _____

WEDDING PACKAGE OVERVIEW:

EST PRICE: _____

INCLUSIONS:	YES ✓	NO ✓	COST:
DUPLICATES/COPIES:			
PHOTO MONTAGE:			
MUSIC ADDED:			
EDITING:			

TOTAL COST: _____

NOTES:

DJ/Entertainment

DJ/LIVE BAND/ENTERTAINMENT:

PHONE: _____   COMPANY: _____

EMAIL: _____   ADDRESS: _____

START TIME: _____   END TIME: _____

ENTERTAINMENT SERVICE OVERVIEW:

EST PRICE: _____

INCLUSIONS:	YES ✓	NO ✓	COST:
SOUND EQUIPMENT:			
LIGHTING:			
SPECIAL EFFECTS:			
GRATUITIES			

TOTAL COST: _____

NOTES:

Florist

FLORIST:

PHONE: _____   COMPANY: _____

EMAIL: _____   ADDRESS: _____

FLORAL PACKAGE:

EST PRICE: _____

INCLUSIONS:	YES ✓	NO ✓	COST:
BRIDAL BOUQUET:			
THROW AWAY BOUQUET:			
CORSAGES:			
CEREMONY FLOWERS			
CENTERPIECES			
CAKE TOPPER			
BOUTONNIERE			

TOTAL COST:

Wedding Cake/ Baker

PHONE: _____   COMPANY: _____

EMAIL: _____   ADDRESS: _____

WEDDING CAKE PACKAGE:

COST: _____   FREE TASTING: _____   DELIVERY FEE: _____

FLAVOR: _____

FILLING: _____

SIZE: _____

SHAPE: _____

COLOR: _____

EXTRAS: _____

TOTAL COST: _____

NOTES:

Transportation Planner

TO CEREMONY: PICK UP TIME: PICK UP LOCATION:

BRIDE:

GROOM:

BRIDE'S PARENTS:

GROOM'S PARENTS:

BRIDESMAIDS:

GROOMSMEN:

NOTES:

TO RECEPTION: PICK UP TIME: PICK UP LOCATION:

BRIDE & GROOM:

BRIDE'S PARENTS:

GROOM'S PARENTS:

BRIDESMAIDS:

GROOMSMEN:

Wedding Planner

BACHELORETTE PARTY:

DATE: _____   LOCATION: _____

TIME: _____   NUMBER OF GUESTS: _____

NOTES:

BACHELOR PARTY:

DATE: _____   LOCATION: _____

TIME: _____   NUMBER OF GUESTS: _____

NOTES:

CEREMONY REHEARSAL:

DATE: _____   LOCATION: _____

TIME: _____   NUMBER OF GUESTS: _____

NOTES:

Wedding Planner

REHEARSAL DINNER:

DATE: _____

LOCATION: _____

TIME: _____

NUMBER OF GUESTS: _____

NOTES:

RECEPTION:

DATE: _____

LOCATION: _____

TIME: _____

NUMBER OF GUESTS: _____

NOTES:

REMINDERS:

_____

_____

_____

_____

_____

Names & Addresses

CEREMONY:

PHONE: _____   CONTACT NAME: _____

EMAIL: _____   ADDRESS: _____

RECEPTION:

PHONE: _____   CONTACT NAME: _____

EMAIL: _____   ADDRESS: _____

OFFICIANT:

PHONE: _____   CONTACT NAME: _____

EMAIL: _____   ADDRESS: _____

WEDDING PLANNER:

PHONE: _____   CONTACT NAME: _____

EMAIL: _____   ADDRESS: _____

CATERER:

PHONE: _____   CONTACT NAME: _____

EMAIL: _____   ADDRESS: _____

FLORIST:

PHONE: _____   CONTACT NAME: _____

EMAIL: _____   ADDRESS: _____

Names & Addresses

BAKERY:

PHONE: _____   CONTACT NAME: _____

EMAIL: _____   ADDRESS: _____

BRIDAL SHOP:

PHONE: _____   CONTACT NAME: _____

EMAIL: _____   ADDRESS: _____

PHOTOGRAPHER:

PHONE: _____   CONTACT NAME: _____

EMAIL: _____   ADDRESS: _____

VIDEOGRAPHER:

PHONE: _____   CONTACT NAME: _____

EMAIL: _____   ADDRESS: _____

DJ/ENTERTAINMENT:

PHONE: _____   CONTACT NAME: _____

EMAIL: _____   ADDRESS: _____

HAIR/NAIL SALON:

PHONE: _____   CONTACT NAME: _____

EMAIL: _____   ADDRESS: _____

Names & Addresses

MAKE UP ARTIST:

PHONE: _____   CONTACT NAME: _____

EMAIL: _____   ADDRESS: _____

RENTALS:

PHONE: _____   CONTACT NAME: _____

EMAIL: _____   ADDRESS: _____

HONEYMOON RESORT/HOTEL:

PHONE: _____   CONTACT NAME: _____

EMAIL: _____   ADDRESS: _____

TRANSPORTATION SERVICE:

PHONE: _____   CONTACT NAME: _____

EMAIL: _____   ADDRESS: _____

NOTES:

Caterer Details

CONTACT INFORMATION:

PHONE: _____   CONTACT NAME: _____

EMAIL: _____   ADDRESS: _____

MENU CHOICE #1:

MENU CHOICE #2:

	YES ✓	NO ✓	COST:
BAR INCLUDED:			
CORKAGE FEE:			
HORS D'OEUVRES:			
TAXES INCLUDED:			
GRATUITIES INCLUDED:			

Menu Planner

HORS D'OEUVRES

1st COURSE:

2nd COURSE:

3rd COURSE:

4th COURSE:

DESSERT:

1 Week Before

	THINGS TO DO:	NOTES:
MONDAY		
TUESDAY		
WEDNESDAY		
THURSDAY		

REMINDERS & NOTES:

1 Week Before

	THINGS TO DO:	NOTES:
FRIDAY		
SATURDAY		
SUNDAY		

LEFT TO DO:

REMINDERS:

NOTES:

Wedding Guest List

NAME:	ADDRESS:	# IN PARTY:	RSVP: ✓

Wedding Guest List

NAME:	ADDRESS:	# IN PARTY:	RSVP: ✓

Wedding Guest List

NAME:	ADDRESS:	# IN PARTY:	RSVP: ✓

Wedding Guest List

NAME:	ADDRESS:	# IN PARTY:	RSVP: ✓

Wedding Guest List

NAME:	ADDRESS:	# IN PARTY:	RSVP: ✓

Wedding Guest List

NAME:	ADDRESS:	# IN PARTY:	RSVP: ✓

Wedding Guest List

NAME:	ADDRESS:	# IN PARTY:	RSVP: ✓

Wedding Guest List

NAME:	ADDRESS:	# IN PARTY:	RSVP: ✓

Wedding Guest List

NAME:	ADDRESS:	# IN PARTY:	RSVP: ✓

Wedding Guest List

NAME:	ADDRESS:	# IN PARTY:	RSVP: ✓

Wedding Guest List

NAME:	ADDRESS:	# IN PARTY:	RSVP: ✓

Wedding Guest List

NAME:	ADDRESS:	# IN PARTY:	RSVP: ✓

Wedding Guest List

NAME:	ADDRESS:	# IN PARTY:	RSVP: ✓

Wedding Guest List

NAME:	ADDRESS:	# IN PARTY:	RSVP: ✓

Wedding Guest List

NAME:	ADDRESS:	# IN PARTY:	RSVP: ✓

Wedding Guest List

NAME:	ADDRESS:	# IN PARTY:	RSVP: ✓

Wedding Guest List

NAME:	ADDRESS:	# IN PARTY:	RSVP: ✓

Wedding Guest List

NAME:	ADDRESS:	# IN PARTY:	RSVP: ✓

Wedding Guest List

NAME:	ADDRESS:	# IN PARTY:	RSVP: ✓

Wedding Guest List

NAME:	ADDRESS:	# IN PARTY:	RSVP: ✓

Wedding Guest List

NAME:	ADDRESS:	# IN PARTY:	RSVP: ✓

Wedding Guest List

NAME:	ADDRESS:	# IN PARTY:	RSVP: ✓

Wedding Guest List

NAME:	ADDRESS:	# IN PARTY:	RSVP: ✓

Wedding Guest List

NAME:	ADDRESS:	# IN PARTY:	RSVP: ✓

Wedding Guest List

NAME:	ADDRESS:	# IN PARTY:	RSVP: ✓

Wedding Guest List

NAME:	ADDRESS:	# IN PARTY:	RSVP: ✓

Wedding Guest List

NAME:	ADDRESS:	# IN PARTY:	RSVP: ✓

Wedding Guest List

NAME:	ADDRESS:	# IN PARTY:	RSVP: ✓

Wedding Guest List

NAME:	ADDRESS:	# IN PARTY:	RSVP: ✓

Wedding Guest List

NAME:	ADDRESS:	# IN PARTY:	RSVP: ✓

Wedding Guest List

NAME:	ADDRESS:	# IN PARTY:	RSVP: ✓

Wedding Guest List

NAME:	ADDRESS:	# IN PARTY:	RSVP: ✓

Seating Chart Planner

Table #

Table #

Table #

Table #

SEATING PLANNER NOTES:

Seating Chart Planner

Table #

Table #

Table #

Table #

SEATING PLANNER NOTES:

Seating Chart Planner

Table #

Table #

Table #

Table #

SEATING PLANNER NOTES:

Seating Chart Planner

Table #

Table #

Table #

Table #

SEATING PLANNER NOTES:

Seating Chart Planner

Table #

Table #

Table #

Table #

SEATING PLANNER NOTES:

Seating Chart Planner

Table #

Table #

Table #

Table #

SEATING PLANNER NOTES:

Seating Chart Planner

Table #

Table #

Table #

Table #

SEATING PLANNER NOTES:

Seating Chart Planner

Table #

Table #

Table #

Table #

SEATING PLANNER NOTES:

Seating Chart Planner

Table #

Table #

Table #

Table #

SEATING PLANNER NOTES:

Seating Chart Planner

Table #

Table #

Table #

Table #

SEATING PLANNER NOTES:

Seating Chart Planner

Table #

Table #

Table #

Table #

SEATING PLANNER NOTES:

Seating Chart Planner

Table #

Table #

Table #

Table #

SEATING PLANNER NOTES:

Seating Chart Planner

Table #

Table #

Table #

Table #

SEATING PLANNER NOTES:

Seating Chart Planner

Table #

Table #

Table #

Table #

SEATING PLANNER NOTES:

Seating Chart Planner

Table #

Table #

Table #

Table #

SEATING PLANNER NOTES:

Seating Chart Planner

Table #

Table #

Table #

Table #

SEATING PLANNER NOTES:

Seating Chart Planner

Table #

Table #

Table #

Table #

SEATING PLANNER NOTES:

Seating Chart Planner

Table #

Table #

Table #

Table #

SEATING PLANNER NOTES:

Seating Chart Planner

Table #

Table #

Table #

Table #

SEATING PLANNER NOTES:

Seating Chart Planner

Table #

Table #

Table #

Table #

SEATING PLANNER NOTES:

Seating Chart Planner

Table #

Table #

Table #

Table #

SEATING PLANNER NOTES:

Seating Chart Planner

Table #

Table #

Table #

Table #

SEATING PLANNER NOTES:

Seating Chart Planner

Table #

Table #

Table #

Table #

SEATING PLANNER NOTES:

Seating Chart Planner

Table #

Table #

Table #

Table #

SEATING PLANNER NOTES:

Seating Chart Planner

Table #

Table #

Table #

Table #

SEATING PLANNER NOTES:

Seating Chart Planner

Table #

Table #

Table #

Table #

SEATING PLANNER NOTES:

Seating Chart Planner

Table #

Table #

Table #

Table #

SEATING PLANNER NOTES:

Seating Chart Planner

Table #

Table #

Table #

Table #

SEATING PLANNER NOTES:

Seating Chart Planner

Table #

Table #

Table #

Table #

SEATING PLANNER NOTES:

Seating Chart Planner

Table #

Table #

Table #

Table #

SEATING PLANNER NOTES:

Seating Chart Planner

Table #

Table #

Table #

Table #

SEATING PLANNER NOTES:

Seating Chart Planner

Table #

Table #

Table #

Table #

SEATING PLANNER NOTES:

Seating Chart Planner

Table #

Table #

Table #

Table #

SEATING PLANNER NOTES:

Seating Chart Planner

Table #

Table #

Table #

Table #

SEATING PLANNER NOTES:

additional notes

additional notes

additional notes

additional notes

additional notes

additional notes

additional notes

additional notes

additional notes

additional notes

additional notes

additional notes

additional notes

additional notes

additional notes

additional notes

additional notes

additional notes

additional notes

additional notes